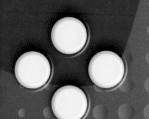

Minecraft Dungeons:

DLC

T0061951

Eyes of Ender
onghold

NETHER WASTES

NEW
10 MISSIONS

VIEW NEXT G

rds   7

cations   2

nder

21st Century Skills **INNOVATION LIBRARY**

Josh Gregory

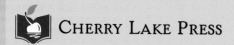

Published in the United States of America by Cherry Lake Publishing Group
Ann Arbor, Michigan
www.cherrylakepublishing.com

Reading Adviser: Beth Walker Gambro, MS, Ed., Reading Consultant, Yorkville, IL

Cherry Lake Press is an imprint of Cherry Lake Publishing Group.

Library of Congress Cataloging-in-Publication Data has been filed and is available at catalog.loc.gov

Cherry Lake Publishing Group would like to acknowledge the work of the Partnership for 21st Century Learning, a Network of Battelle for Kids. Please visit http://www.battelleforkids.org/networks/p21 for more information.

Printed in the United States of America
Corporate Graphics

Josh Gregory is the author of more than 200 books for kids. He has written about everything from animals to technology to history. A graduate of the University of Missouri–Columbia, he currently lives in Chicago, Illinois.

Contents

CHAPTER 1

A Growing World

If you've ever played *Minecraft*, you know that it's a truly huge video game. Its biggest fans have been playing for years and years without ever running out of things to do. There are always new places to explore and new things to build.

In 2020, Mojang, the creators of *Minecraft*, released a new game called *Minecraft Dungeons*. While not quite as massive as the original game, it is still a very big game with a lot to do. There are tons of unique levels to explore, cool gear to discover, and enemies to battle. To uncover everything the game has to offer would take dozens and dozens of hours. However, dedicated fans are always willing to push a game to its limits. They play as long as necessary to see and do everything in a game. But what comes next after they've exhausted their favorite game's deepest secrets?

Before high-speed internet was common, **developers** would sometimes create something called expansion packs for their most popular games. These were discs that could be purchased at stores just like regular games. They required players to own the original game, and they added more features and content.

These days, it is much more common for developers to extend the life of their games by offering downloadable content, or DLC. Sometimes DLC is free and automatically sent out to all players. For example,

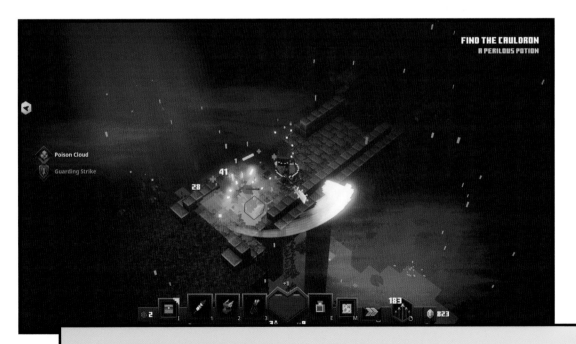

Minecraft Dungeons started out with plenty of content to keep players busy for a long time, but DLC has made it even more massive.

The Story Continues

The original *Minecraft Dungeons* campaign tells the story of the Arch-Illager, an everyday villager who turns evil after discovering a magic object called the Orb of Dominance. It is up to players to chase down the Arch-Illager and save the people of the *Minecraft* world from his evil plans.

Each DLC pack in *Minecraft Dungeons* tells a short story of its own, almost like a miniature campaign. These DLC stories are set after the events of the main game's campaign and continue that storyline. So if you are interested in the story and want to avoid spoilers, you should be sure to play the main campaign and DLC packs in the order they were released.

a game like *Fortnite* is always changing as new updates are released. This keeps things fresh for even the most seasoned veterans of the game.

Other times, developers choose to create DLC that adds on to the original game. Usually, this type of DLC costs money. It might be a huge addition to the game that costs almost as much as an entire game on its own. Or it could come in the form of smaller DLC packs that can be purchased as **microtransactions**.

So far, there have been six packs of DLC released for *Minecraft Dungeons*. Each one offers a few new levels to explore, along with new gear to find and new enemies to battle. Most also have some twists to the core *Minecraft Dungeons* gameplay to keep experienced players on their toes. There are also **cosmetic** items included with each pack, so players can change the looks of their characters.

Each DLC pack can be purchased separately as a microtransaction for a few dollars. However, there are also other ways to get the DLC in larger chunks. The Hero Pass will give you access to the first two DLC

Skip

The story of the Arch-Illager continues beyond the ending of *Minecraft Dungeons* and into the game's six DLC packs.

The *Minecraft Dungeons* DLC will send you to dangerous areas unlike anything in the main game.

packs, *Jungle Awakens* and *Creeping Winter*, as well as some special cosmetic items. The Season Pass bundles the next four DLC packs together. If you don't have the main game yet, you can get the Ultimate Edition, which contains *Minecraft Dungeons* and all of the DLC that has been released so far. And if you have the main game already but want all the DLC, you can get the Ultimate DLC Bundle, which groups all of the game's DLC together. This might all sound confusing, but it's actually a fairly flexible system that lets players pick and choose which content they want.

Any time you buy DLC for *Minecraft Dungeons*, you are only buying it for one version of the game. For example, if you buy DLC for the PlayStation 4 version of the game, you won't be able to use it on the PC version of the game. This is an important thing to keep in mind if you play on multiple types of gaming systems.

Are you ready to see what awaits beyond the end of the original *Minecraft Dungeons* campaign? Even if you think you're a *Minecraft Dungeons* pro, you might be surprised at how many new features the game's DLC has to offer.

In the DLC, you'll get to do things that are impossible in the main game, such as flying through the sky.

CHAPTER 2

Heading to the Island Realms

The first *Minecraft Dungeons* DLC pack, *Jungle Awakens*, was released on July 1, 2020, just a few weeks after the launch of the main game. This pack has a jungle theme and adds three new missions to the game: Dingy Jungle, Panda Plateau, and Overgrown Temple.

These three levels offer a lot of new ground to cover. But they are more than just new spaces. They also contain completely different enemies from the ones seen in the main game. Among them are moss-covered skeletons and vines that pop up from the ground. Wild animals such as ocelots and pandas wander through the levels, helping to create a rich jungle setting.

New gear in *Jungle Awakens* includes the ocelot armor, which not only grants protection but also lets players dress their characters like ocelots. There are even new food and potions to find. Enemies drop slices of melon, which can quickly heal your character's health. You might also discover oakwood brew, which grants extra defense for 15 seconds.

To access *Jungle Awakens*, visit the Mission Select screen in camp. Then choose to travel to the Island Realms. This will bring you to a new map different from

The Island Realms map is a huge area where you'll find most of the game's DLC levels.

Try to avoid falling into cold water in *Creeping Winter*. It'll turn you into an ice cube!

the one in the main *Minecraft Dungeons* campaign. One of the islands is the jungle world of the first DLC pack, and you can start the first mission from there.

The next DLC pack to be released was *Creeping Winter*, on September 8. As its title promises, this pack has an icy winter theme. Like *Jungle Awakens*, it can be accessed by visiting the Island Realms from the Mission

Select screen. You will see an icy island on the map, and this is where the adventure begins.

The three new areas in *Creeping Winter* are called Frosted Fjord, Lone Fortress, and Lost Settlement. As you journey across these new locations, you'll encounter snow, ice, and freezing-cold water. You'll even visit a frozen village area. Be careful, though. These missions contain new threats that aren't in previous areas of the game. For example, when walking on ice, your character will slide around, making

When to Begin

Once you have installed a DLC pack, you are able to start playing the new levels whenever you want to. For players who are following the game's story, it makes sense to play everything in order. But for those who are just interested in battling, exploring, and searching for loot, things are more open-ended.

You can feel free to dive into the new levels whenever you like, even if you haven't finished the main game. However, you might want to hold off anyway unless you are very confident in your character's strength. Some of the challenges in the game's DLC levels are much tougher than what you'll find in the main game.

it difficult to get where you want to go. And if you fall in the water, your character will briefly be encased in a block of ice. You'll need to press a button quickly to break free and continue adventuring.

Seek out new items like the ice wand. This artifact allows you to stun enemies with a special ice attack. You can also find the snow armor, which offers extra protection against ice attacks. This will come in handy as you make your way through *Creeping Winter*.

In *Howling Peaks*, you'll be able to see the powerful bursts of wind that can knock you off ledges.

Creeping Winter also adds some new food and a new type of potion. Enemies will drop cooked salmon, which helps you restore health, though not as quickly as the melon from *Jungle Awakens*. You should also try to track down the sweet brew potion, which offers extra protection against freezing attacks. This is especially useful when going up against new enemies like the iceologer or the frozen zombie, which specialize in icy attacks. Another new enemy to watch out for is the illusioner. This tricky foe can blind your character, which makes about half your attacks miss for a few seconds.

Howling Peaks, the game's third DLC pack, was released on December 9. This one sends players into a dangerous mountain region. Mountain goats and llamas roam the area. Just like the first two DLC packs, the new mountainous levels are located on a new island in the Island Realms map. Its new areas are called Windswept Peaks, Gale Sanctum, and Colossal Rampart. As you make your way up the mountain, you'll battle across a hidden temple, the walls of a huge fortress, and a windy wilderness area.

Watch out for wind as you explore the levels of *Howling Peaks*. It can push your character off ledges. And because you're climbing a mountain, there are a lot of ledges. Many of them are very high. This means a wind burst hitting you at the wrong time can cause serious damage! You'll also need to use wind to solve puzzles and open doors.

Many of the DLC's new enemies also use wind-based attacks. If you want to protect yourself against these threats, try looking for the new dense brew potion. This

Cute mountain goats wander all around the levels of *Howling Peaks*.

OPEN THE CAVE PASS - 0/2
WELCOME TO WINDSWEPT PEAKS

DENSE BREW

Grants resistance to pushbacks and
melee damage.

12,064

A dense brew can make navigating *Howling Peaks* much simpler, but it only lasts for a short while.

helps keep your character standing steady in the face of strong winds. You can also try to find the new climbing gear armor. It has the same effect, but it will never wear off as long as you have it equipped.

You should also keep an eye out for enemies to drop sweet berries. This new food item will only heal your character a little bit. However, it will also give you a very large boost of speed for a few seconds. This will give you a big advantage in combat.

CHAPTER 3

Exploring Other Dimensions

By the end of 2020, *Minecraft* fans had gotten the chance to play *Minecraft Dungeons* and its first three DLC packs. But Mojang was not done with its spree of new releases. Another three DLC packs were also released in 2021, ensuring that *Minecraft Dungeons* fans would have no reason to get bored anytime soon.

The first DLC of the year was called *Flames of the Nether*. Released on February 24, it takes place in the Nether, an area that was familiar to longtime fans of the original *Minecraft*. This dangerous, lava-filled area is located in a different dimension from the main world of *Minecraft*. To access it in *Minecraft Dungeons*, you'll need to visit the Mission Select screen and then choose to travel to Other Dimensions. This will bring you to a new map different from the main campaign or the Island Realms.

Flames of the Nether has more new areas than any *Minecraft Dungeons* DLC pack released so far. Its six new locations are called Nether Wastes, Basalt Deltas, Warped Forest, Nether Fortress, Crimson Forest, and Soul Sand Valley. They are packed with fire, lava, and other hazards you'll need to navigate if you want to make it through safely.

New enemies such as the blaze will use fire attacks against you, so be sure to prepare properly before you

FIND THE NEXT PORTAL
CRIMSON FOREST

In the Crimson Forest, almost everything is burning red.

dive into the Nether. Try equipping armor that protects against fire damage. You'll also run into enemies like wither skeletons. These foes use attacks that cause your character to become withered. This will cause your character to take damage every few moments until the effect wears off. The amount of damage will increase over time, so be sure to keep an eye on your health if your character gets hit with one of these attacks.

Recharge your breath at every opportunity as you explore the levels of *Hidden Depths*.

The fifth DLC pack, *Hidden Depths*, was released on May 26, 2021—exactly one year after the release of the main *Minecraft Dungeons* game. This DLC pack marks a return to the Island Realms map. It takes place in three underwater locations near a group of islands on the map. They are called Coral Rise, Abyssal Monument, and Radiant Ravine. Though this DLC returns to just three missions after the six new locations of *Flames of the Nether*, each one is much larger than the typical *Minecraft Dungeons* mission.

When you start playing *Hidden Depths*, you'll notice right away that things are a little different than you are used to in the rest of *Minecraft Dungeons*. First of all, you'll see that your health meter is now split into two sides: a red one and a blue one. The red one tracks your character's health, just like normal. But the blue side tracks your character's breath. This will slowly go down as you explore and battle through the *Hidden Depths* locations. If it runs out, your character will take damage. To replenish it, seek out air vents. These are small platforms where bubbles rise up from the ocean floor. Standing on one will refill your blue breath meter. There are also other new tools to help keep your breath meter full. Enemies will drop potions of water breathing, which stop your breath meter from dropping for a little while. You can also find an item called a conduit. This is an object you can pick up and carry around, then drop it wherever you like. It creates a large air bubble around itself. As long as you are holding it or standing near it, your breath meter will not fall.

You will also move slower while underwater, and so will your ranged attacks. Your dodge roll move will also be replaced with a new dash move, which gives you a

Blazing a Trail

If you've spent much time playing *Minecraft Dungeons*, you know that each level's difficulty can be adjusted before you start playing. Usually, players try to conquer the highest difficulties they can. This gives them better gear and more experience points. It is also lots of fun to enjoy the challenge of the game.

Sometimes you might just want to check out all of a DLC pack's levels as soon as possible. Or maybe you want to see which kinds of new enemies and gear are available in different levels before you invest the time in conquering higher difficulties. Don't be afraid to turn down the difficulty and blaze through DLC levels on your first playthrough. This will let you open up the game's map without any trouble. Then you can go back to play the parts that interest you most.

brief boost of speed. All of this means the game's controls will feel a lot different when playing in underwater areas, so it will take some getting used to.

The final DLC pack to date, *Echoing Void*, was released on July 28, 2021. This one will take you to The End, the home of the dangerous foes known as Endermen. It adds three large areas called The Stronghold, End

The levels of *Echoing Void* are some of the strangest and most difficult in *Minecraft Dungeons*.

Wilds, and Broken Citadel. Accessing these new areas is a little more complex than it was in previous DLC packs. First, you'll need to revisit six of the locations from the original *Minecraft Dungeons* campaign. They are:

- Pumpkin Pastures
- Highblock Halls
- Soggy Swamp
- Desert Temple
- Cacti Canyon
- Creeper Woods

Each Eye of Ender is hidden away in a secret area and is guarded by a very tough enemy, so tracking them all down is no simple task.

If you have *Echoing Void*, each of these locations will now have a new secret area you'll need to explore. Once you find it, you'll have to battle a powerful enemy called an Endersent to earn an Eye of Ender. You'll need all six Eyes of Ender to continue with the DLC. Once you have them, visit the new location called The Stronghold. It is located in the bottom right of the map screen on the main Mission Select screen. Inside The Stronghold, you'll eventually reach a place where you can use the Eyes of Ender to unlock a portal to The End. This will immediately take you to the DLC's second location, End Wilds. From here on, you can simply go to the Other Dimensions map on the Mission Select screen to play End Wilds or the final *Echoing Void* area, Broken Citadel.

As with the other DLC packs, Broken Citadel will give you a chance to find lots of new gear and face off against new enemies. But even more exciting than that, you'll get the chance to fly! At certain points in the new levels, you can launch your character into the sky and soar across the map.

CHAPTER 4

The Adventure Never Ends

Paid DLC packs aren't the only way to get more out of *Minecraft Dungeons*. The developers also release plenty of free content that anyone who owns the original game can enjoy. Much of the time, this content is released at the same time as the bigger paid packs.

Sometimes this new content is similar to what gets added through the paid DLC packs. For example, at the same time *Jungle Awakens* was released, a new area was also added to the main *Minecraft Dungeons* campaign for free. Called Lower Temple, it was a hidden area accessed through the main campaign's Desert Temple location. Inside, players could discover two entirely new weapons, the battlestaff and the dual crossbows.

Other free content adds new features that players can enjoy across the main campaign or DLC. For example, when *Flames of the Nether* was released, there were also several major features added to the game for all players. From then on, players could choose to try to hunt down special enemies called ancient mobs. Doing this allows them to earn gold, a new form of money in the game. Gold can be spent at a new merchant who shows up in camp to sell special "gilded" items. Gilded

Sometimes entire levels are added to *Minecraft Dungeons* and are completely free for all players to enjoy.

items are some of the most powerful gear in the game. This meant the new features were perfect for players who already had very powerful characters and still wanted more from the game.

Of course, a big part of the fun in *Minecraft Dungeons* is teaming up with friends to explore and battle

The battles in the DLC levels can be especially tough, so it never hurts to bring a buddy along to help out.

ONWARDS AND UPWARDS
THE ROOF OF THE WORLD

GROWING STAFF
UNIQUE 34

No matter how you're experiencing the DLC, you'll always get to keep all the gear you find.

enemies. But what happens if one player has purchased all of the DLC and another hasn't? Or what if several friends have all purchased different DLC packs? *Minecraft Dungeons* makes it as simple as possible for friends to keep playing together in these situations.

Whichever player is the host of a game is the one whose DLC can be played in a multiplayer match. For example, if the host player has *Echoing Void*, other players can still join in and enjoy the new levels even if they don't own the DLC. But they will only be able to play it while connected to the host's multiplayer session. The really great part is that players can still keep any gear they find while playing DLC hosted by another player. That means you could end up with new kinds of items without ever actually purchasing the DLC.

Looking Ahead

As of early 2022, Mojang has not announced any further plans for *Minecraft Dungeons* DLC. However, that doesn't mean that it won't happen. Some games continue to receive new DLC updates for years and years after they are released. If a game is popular enough, developers will continue supporting it long into the future. But even if *Minecraft Dungeons* never receives another major update again, players should have plenty to keep them busy for a very long time!

If you want the best gear *Minecraft Dungeons* has to offer, you'll need to try the DLC packs at some point.

Between the main campaign, all six DLC packs, and the free content released so far, *Minecraft Dungeons* players should never have any trouble staying busy. So if you're ready for adventure, get out there and start exploring!

GLOSSARY

campaign (kam-PAYN) a set of levels or missions in a video game that are meant to be played in a certain order, often to tell a story

cosmetic (kahz-MEH-tik) relating to how something looks

developers (dih-VEL-uh-purz) people who make video games or other computer programs

microtransactions (MYE-kroh-trans-ak-shuhns) things that can be purchased for a small amount of money within a video game or other computer program

FIND OUT MORE

Books

Milton, Stephanie. *Guide to Minecraft Dungeons: A Handbook for Heroes*. New York: Del Rey, 2020.

Zeiger, Jennifer. *The Making of Minecraft*. Ann Arbor, MI: Cherry Lake Publishing, 2017.

Websites

Minecraft Dungeons
https://www.minecraft.net/en-us/about-dungeons
Check out the official *Minecraft Dungeons* website for the latest updates on the game.

Minecraft Dungeons Wiki
https://minecraft.fandom.com/wiki/Minecraft_Dungeons
This fan-created wiki is packed with useful details about *Minecraft Dungeons* and its DLC.

INDEX